CW01183502

Copyright 2013

Knitted designs by Joan Gallup Grimord
Design Contributor - Monique Grimord
Interior Photography by Lindsey Clark
Illustrations - Joan Gallup Grimord

Every effort has been made to present accurate instructions for making these animals. This author however, cannot accept responsibility for any written errors made, or any misinterpretation of instructions.

Table of Contents

About Miniature Knitting	4-5
Supplies needed	6
Techniques for completing projects	7-14
Teddy Bear	16
Lady Bug	19
Donkey	21
Giraffe	24
Dachshund	27
Elephant	29
Octopus	31
Dinosaur	33
Hippo	36
Kittens	39
Spotted Dog	43
Turtle	46
Panda Pair	49
Kangaroo	52
Glossary of Terms	56
Suppliers	57

About Miniature Knitting

One Christmas, when I was a young girl, our family received a small package in the mail for Christmas. Unwrapping the package revealed an unusual ornament to hang on the tree. A unique pair of forest green mittens tied together with a little red ribbon, hand knitted, and only about one and a quarter inches tall. There was a white snowflake pattern across the top of the mittens with a tiny protruding thumb on the side of each one. I marveled at the fact that they were so tiny and well crafted at the same time. How could this be? They were only 1 1/4" long! I was fascinated with the tiny size and the mystery of how they could have been made. I had to try myself.

I was born with a creative drive, and I immediately went home and began the effort. I pulled out two pins and sewing thread frow my mom's drawer, and with my industrious little mind and fingers began to make my own pair. Sadly, I had no success in my endeavors. My fingers felt like the biggest plums in the world. It seemed impossible. Did elves actuallly make them? I was forever daunted by the mystery of the miniature mittens.

That is, until I was an adult and upon inquiry learned that Miniture Knitting is done with regular, though thin, sized knitting needles, not pins! I soon discovered a whole world out there of miniature makers and lots of information about working in miniature. I found a book on the subject of miniature knitting and that was the start of a whole new adventure. I took a class at the Guild School in Maine, taught by master knitter, Sue Ressequie, who introduced her students to techniques that make knitting in miniature easier than ever. It is in thanks to her shared knowledge that I dedicate this book. After learning techniques in her class I went back home inspired to design my own animals.

This book contains instructions for making 14 little animals. It will discuss the tools and supplies needed for miniature knitting. Knitting techniques for each step are discussed along with detailed illlustrations for guidance. A glossary of terms is provided at the end of the book, along with sources for supplies. I hope you find as much pleasure from making these projects as I have found in designing each knitted toy, and sharing them in this instructional book.

In this book you will learn about:

- tools and supplies
- miniature knitting techniques
- casting on stitches
- pocket knitting
- tube knitting
- M1, adding and decreasing, gathering stitches
- assembling animals

A word of warning: miniature knitting requires patience. There will be some moments of frustration. I often find myself losing a stitch and tearing the whole thing out after spending time on it. The good news is that not much is lost: only a tiny little leg, or a tail. Starting over is easy. So stick with it. You will be rewarded by your endeavors.

Supplies Needed

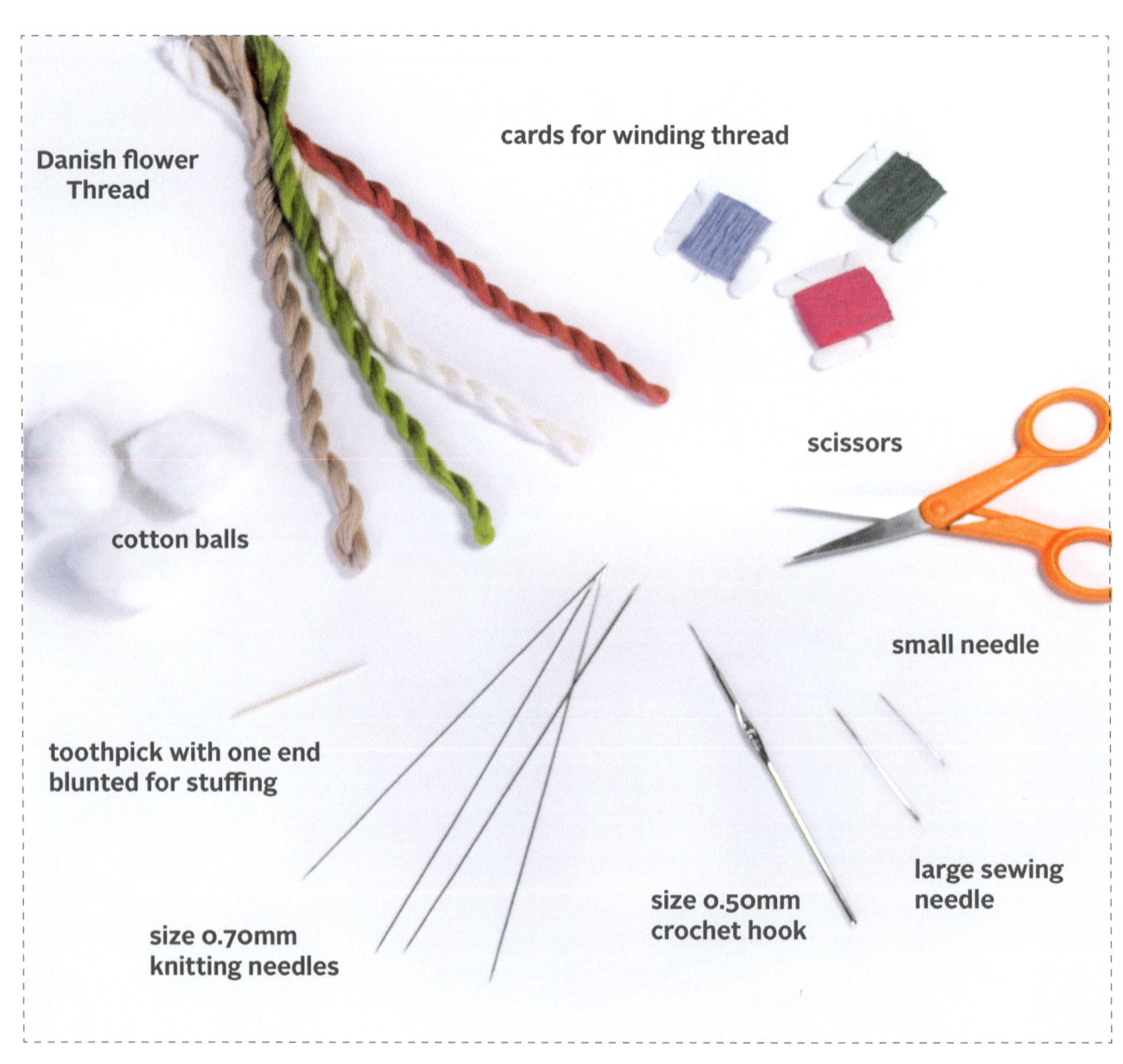

- Danish flower Thread
- cards for winding thread
- cotton balls
- scissors
- small needle
- toothpick with one end blunted for stuffing
- size 0.50mm crochet hook
- large sewing needle
- size 0.70mm knitting needles

Techniques for completing projects

Casting on Stitches using the Knit method

Cast on your stitches using this method for two reasons: first, with this method the cast ons are flexible which is helpful for knitting in miniature. Second, the placement of the starting thread will help you identify whether you are on side A or B when doing double knit pockets. Always leave a tail of about 8" when starting your cast ons, This will come in handy for turning parts inside out.

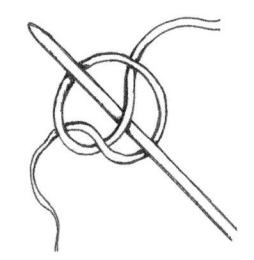

A Make a slip knot on the left needle.

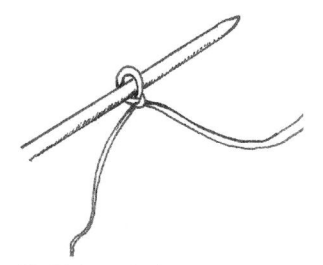

B Tighten the loop.

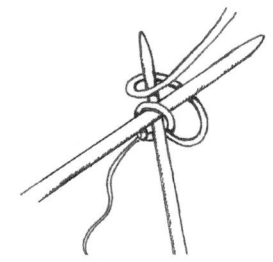

C Knit into the loop.

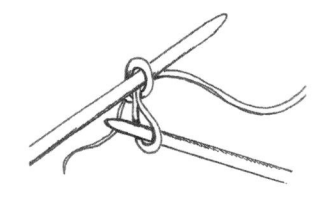

D Pull a loop through.

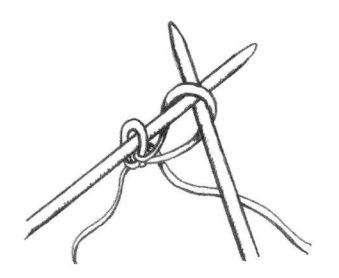

E Place the loop back on the left needle.

F Tighten to create a new stitch. Knit into the new stitch.

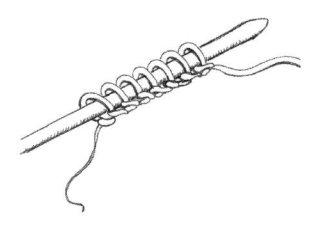

G Repeat to complete the amount of cast ons needed.

Double Knit Pockets

The double knit (DK) pocket technique is used most often for making these animals. The pocket is knitted by alternating the knit stitch and slip stitch across each row. Keep the feed thread behind the right needle when starting a row.

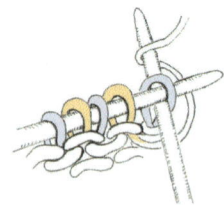

Knit Stitch
Always start a row with the feed thread behind the right needle.

Slip Stitch
Slip the stitch onto the right needle purl-wise keeping the feed thread behind the right needle.

Practice Pocket

1. Cast on 14 stitches leaving a tail of 8" with the starting thread. The first row is called Side A. The starting thread, or tail, hangs on the left side, the feed thread on the right. Knit one, slip one across the row seven times = (K1, S1) x 7. Turn the knitting over and the starting thread (tail) will be on the right side. This is called Side B. Knit one, slip one across the row seven times = (K1, S1) x 7. This completes ONE ROUND. By identifying which side the tail is on you will always be able to determine if you are working side A or B.

2. Repeat (K1, S1) x 7 for six more rounds for total of 7 rounds to complete the pocket. The knit stitches have a tendency to hide behind the slip stitch and you must work to find it. Don't make the mistake of knitting the slip stitch, or slipping the knit stitch. It must be knitted absolutely correctly to create a pocket that opens properly when done. To make sure your pocket remains hollow you can check as you go by poking the interior with a needle and sliding back and forth. If it catches, most likely an error has been made.

The finished pocket
The knit stitches are shown in blue and the slip stitches are orange. The knit stitches tend to hide behind the slips, the slip stitches look like purls.

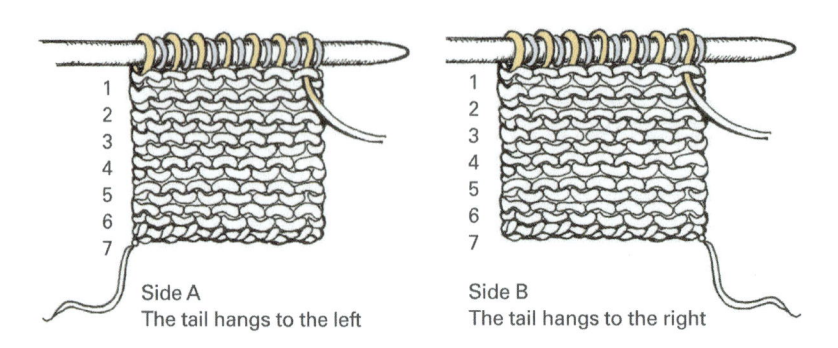

Side A
The tail hangs to the left

Side B
The tail hangs to the right

Removing Double Knit stitches from the needle

This method is referred to as "picking up the stitches Pocket Style". With the sewing needle pick up a knit purl-wise; with the knitting needle pick up a slip purl-wise. Repeat all the way across. Then slide the sewing needle through the rest of the slips remaining on the knitting needle.

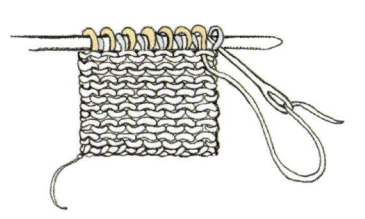

A Pick up a knit stitch wih a threaded needle and remove

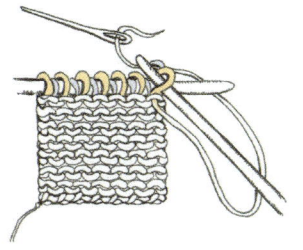

B Pick up the slip stitch with a knitting needle. Alternate all the way across.

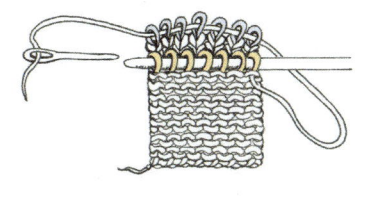

C Now take your sewing needle and pick up the rest of the stitches off the knitting needle.

Turning Double Knit Pockets inside out

Larger pockets can be turned inside out with the blunted toothpick tool easily, but thin pockets for legs can present difficulty. Following these steps makes it easier to turn them inside out.

A Push the eye end of a large needle through the pocket.

B Thread the beginning tail through the needle.

C Pull up through, turning inside out gently. Use your blunted toothpick to push it also.

D When inside out, use the blunted tooth pick to shape the form. Take your fingernail and slide it along the sides to even the knit. Put the needle back up through the pocket and cut the tail thread.

E Stuff if pattern requests it. Pull thread to close the pocket. Knot if pattern requests, if not, it is ready to sew in place.

9

Increasing Stitches on sides of Double Knit Pockets

The patterns for the toys often call for increasing stitches to widen the shape needed. This method is referred to as EI, for End Increase. To do an EI you need to knit a stitch into the base of the 1st stitch on the side. Sometimes the first stitch on your needle will be a knit, other times a slip, depending on the pattern. The standard way of increasing would be to knit into the stitch but I have found that using a crochet hook when making an EI is especially helpful when working in miniature.

EIK › End Increase into the base of a knit stitch:

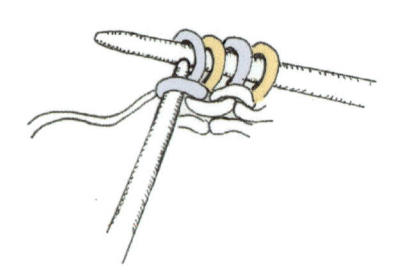

A Turn your knitting around to the back side to see the base of the knit stitch. Loosen the base with your needle, pulling it out.

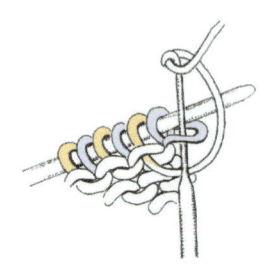

B Turn knitting back to right side. Push the crochet hook through the loosened stitch. Wrap yarn and bring a loop down through base.

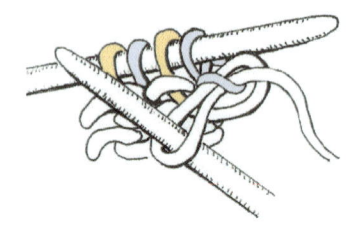

C Put your right needle into the loop, tighten, and you have a new stitch. Correct the tension as you begin the row.

EIS › End Increase into the base of a slip stitch:

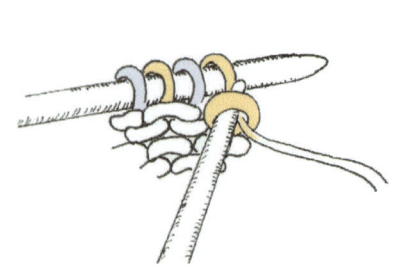

A Loosen the base of the stitch with your knitting needle.

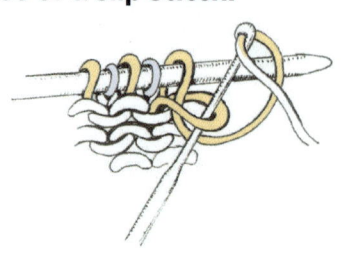

B Put the crochet hook up through the loosened stitch. Wrap yarn and bring a loop down through.

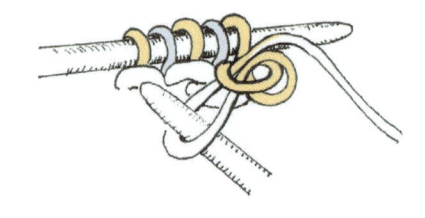

C Put your right needle through the loop, tighten, and you have a new stitch. Correct the tension as you begin the row.

Decreasing Stitches on the sides of Double Knit Pockets

The patterns call for decreasing stiches on the pockets to narrow the forms when needed. When a row starts with a knit, the decrease is called a EDKS: End Decrease, Knit, Slip, pass over. When a row starts with a slip the decrease is called an EDSK : End Decrease, Slip, Knit, pass over.

EDKS

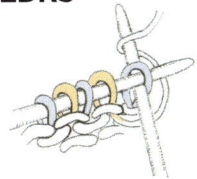

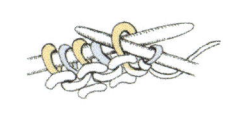

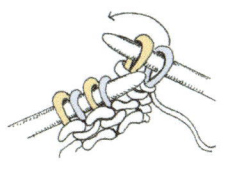

Knit 1

Slip 1

Pass Knit over Slip and off needle

EDSK

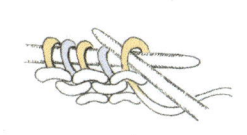

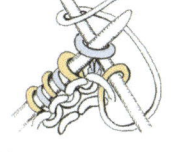

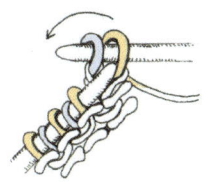

Slip 1

Knit 1

Pass Slip over Knit and off needle

M1 and M1T Stitches

Some patterns in this book will call for increasing stitches within the pocket using M1s or M1Ts.

M1

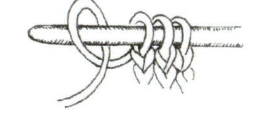

A Twist the thread once to make an M1.

B Slide it onto the needle and gently pull to make a siitch.

M1T

A Twist the thread like an M1.

B Twist the loop again to the right.

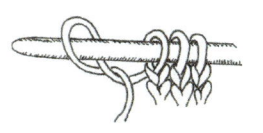

C Slide on needle and gently pull to make a stitch.

11

Tube Knitting

Tubes will consist of 2 to 4 stitches for the purposes in this book. The illustration shown shows three on the needle. After knitting the first row, pull the beginning tail up behind the kniting. Do not turn your knitting over to the other side for the next row, but instead slide the knitting across to the opposite end of the needle, and bring your thread along the back. Knit the next row. Repeat in this manner. When changing colors, do not tie threads, but carry them up through the tube. When complete, with a sewing needle pick up the loops and gather.

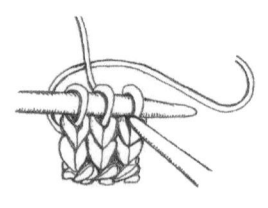

A Carry beginning thread inside tubing. Slide work to the other end of needle. Bring knitting thread around back to begin each new row.

B Thread sewing needle and gather stitches when complete. Snip off beginning thread to hide in tube.

C Pull tight. Roll tubing between fingers to form.

Knit two together

This method makes knitting two together in miniature an easy process.

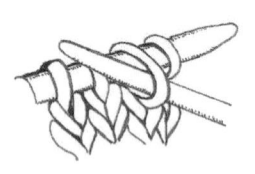

A With your right needle pull the second stitch loose.

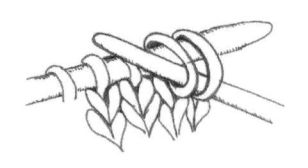

B Now pick up both to loosen them.

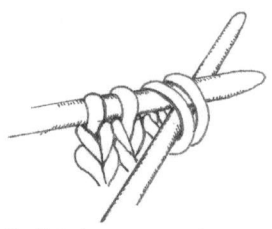

C Knit the two together.

Changing colors

To change colors when Double Knitting, start a round with a new color leaving a 2" end and complete 1/2 of the round. At this point cut the old thread to 2" and tie the two together with a box knot. Then complete the 2nd half of the round. You can cut the threads down to 1/2" after securing them. Sometimes the pattern will ask you not to cut threads if the old color is to be picked up again. In this case, let it lay loosely until used again.

Preparing Ears for sewing to body

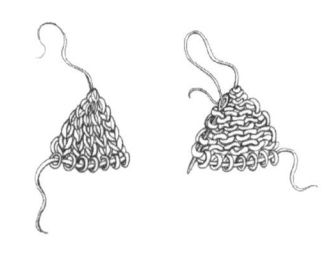

Triangle ear
Thread sewing needle with starting thread at top of ear. Stitch down to base of ear. Sew both ends into body to secure ear.

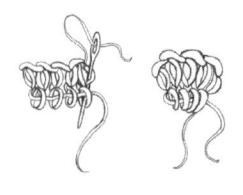

Round ear
Thread sewing needle with starting thread. Stitch down to base. Gather at base to round out ear.

French knot

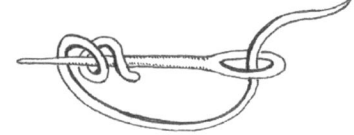

Double Loop
Bring needle up through fabric, wrap the needle with 2 loops.

Wrapping a Triple Loop
Bring needle up through fabric, wrap the needle with 3 loops.

Push needle down through a hole next to first and pull gently to make a knot.

The finished french knot.

Fringe

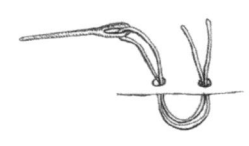

A Bring needle down through and back up to create a loop.

B Bring both ends through loop and pull. Trim.

Assembling the Parts

Forming each part After turning parts inside out and before stuffing, it can help to run your finger nail along the side seams to even up the tension of the knitting. Play with the piece, pulling and shaping until it looks right. Use the blunt end of the toothpick tool to push out areas that need to be formed.

Stuffing Use the pointed side of the toothpick to feed small bits of stuffing into the pockets at a time. Use the blunted side to push it in. Don't over stuff the parts.

Assembly Only knot areas when specified in the pattern. Otherwise a knot will show on such a tiny item. It is best to hide the thread, rather than knotting, when sewing the parts on by going back and forth through the stuffed body until the part is secure and then snip the thread. Simply pull the thread lightly, cut it, and let it pop back into the stuffing to be hidden.

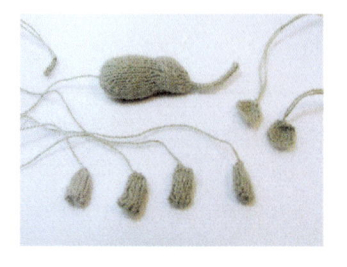

Example of completed parts
These are all parts for the elephant, Stuffed and ready to assemble.

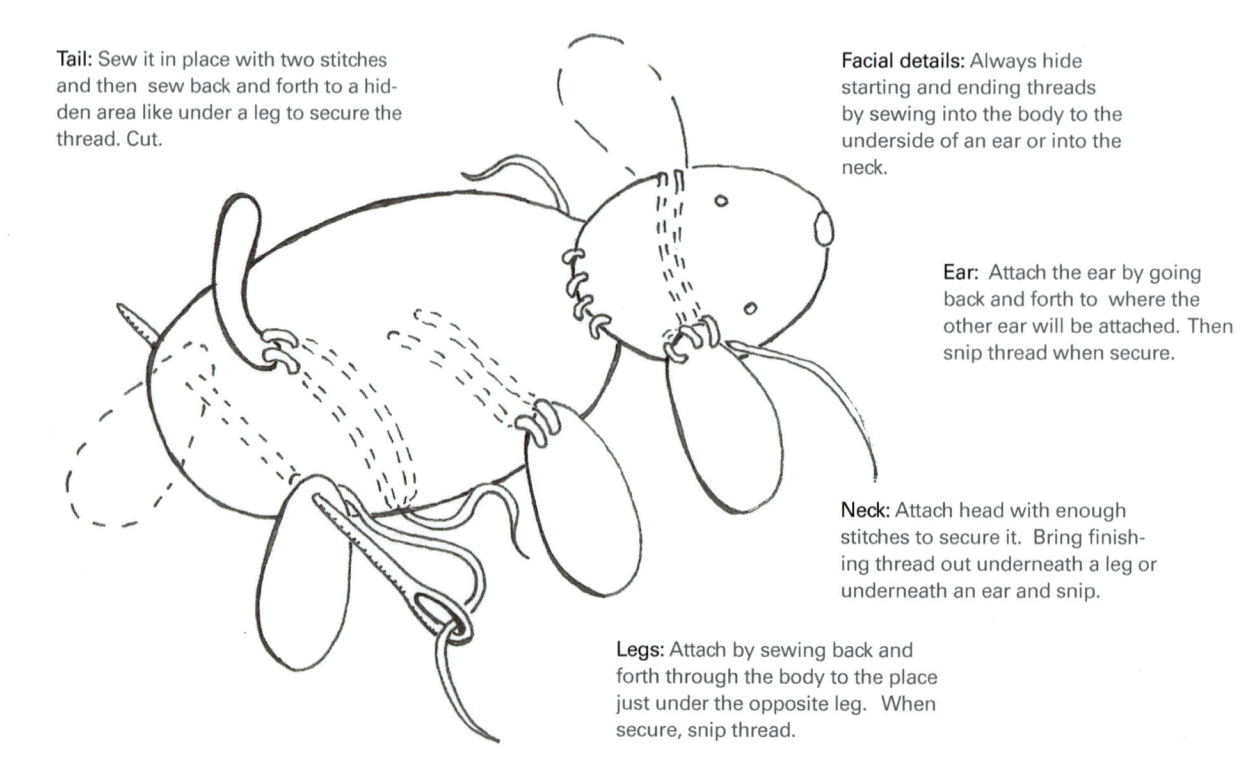

Tail: Sew it in place with two stitches and then sew back and forth to a hidden area like under a leg to secure the thread. Cut.

Facial details: Always hide starting and ending threads by sewing into the body to the underside of an ear or into the neck.

Ear: Attach the ear by going back and forth to where the other ear will be attached. Then snip thread when secure.

Neck: Attach head with enough stitches to secure it. Bring finishing thread out underneath a leg or underneath an ear and snip.

Legs: Attach by sewing back and forth through the body to the place just under the opposite leg. When secure, snip thread.

the *Animals*

Teddy Bear

Colors #705 Brown   DMC black

Head

- Cast on 14 of #705
- DK rounds

Rounds	Side
1, 2	A .. (K1, S1) x 7 B .. (K1, S1) x 7
3	A .. EIK, (K1, S1) x 7 = 15 sts B .. EIK, (K1, S1) x 7, K1 = 16 sts
4, 5	A .. (S1, K1) x 8 B .. (S1, K1) x 8
6	A .. (S1, K1) x 3, S1, M1T, K1, S1, K1, M1T, (S1, K1) x 3 = 18 sts B .. (S1, K1) x 3, (S2, K1) x 2, (S1, K1) x 3
7	A .. (S1, K1) x 3, (S1, K1, M1T, K1) x 2, (S1, K1) x 3 = 20 sts B .. (S1, K1) x 3, (S3, K1) x 2, (S1, K1) x 3
8	A .. (S1, K1) x 3, S1, K1, M1T, K2, S1, K2, M1T, K1, (S1, K1) x 3 = 22 sts B .. (S1, K1) x 3, (S4, K1) x 2, (S1, K1) x 3
9	A .. (S1, K1) x 3, S1, K1, M1T, K3, S1, K3, M1T, K1, (S1, K1) x 3 = 24 sts B .. (S1, K1) x 3, (S5, K1) x 2, (S1, K1) x 3
10, 11	A .. (S1, K1) x 3, (S1, K5) x 2, (S1, K1) x 3 B .. (S1, K1) x 3, (S5, K1) x 2, (S1, K1) x 3
12	A .. (S1, K1) x 3, S1, K2tog, K3, S1, K3, K2tog, (S1, K1) x 3 = 22 sts B .. (S1, K1) x 3, (S4, K1) x 2, (S1, K1) x 3
13	A .. (S1, K1) x 3, S1, K2tog, K2, S1, K2, K2tog, (S1, K1) x 3 = 20 sts B .. (S1, K1) x 3, (S3, K1) x 2, (S1, K1) x 3
14	A .. (S1, K1) x 3, S1, K2tog, K1, S1, K1, K2tog, (S1, K1) x 3 = 18 sts B .. (S1, K1) x 3, (S2, K1) x 2, (S1, K1) x 3
15	A .. (S1, K1) x 3, (S1, K2tog) x 2, (S1, K1) x 3 = 16 sts B .. (S1, K1) x 8

- Cut thread to 8" and pick up stitches with sewing needle pocket style. Turn head inside out. Use the blunt end of your stuffing tool to push out the snout area. Stuff the head and form it so that the snout protrudes. Pull the opening closed and knot. This end will be attached to the bear body.

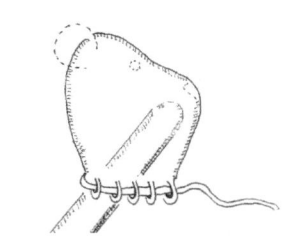

Forming the bear snout

Body

- Cast on 14 of #705
- DK rounds

Rounds	Side
1, 2	A .. (K1, S1) x 7 B .. (K1, S1) x 7
3	A .. EIK, (K1, S1) x 7 = 15 sts B .. EIK, (K1, S1) x 7, K1 = 16 sts
4,5	A .. (S1, K1) x 8 B .. (S1, K1) x 8
6	A .. EIS, (S1, K1) x 8 = 17 sts B .. EIS, (S1, K1) x 8, S1 = 18 sts
7,8	A .. (K1, S1) x 9 B .. (K1, S1) x 9
9	A .. EIK, (K1, S1) x 9 = 19 sts B .. EIK, (K1, S1) x 9, K1 = 20 sts
10	A .. (S1, K1) x 3, (S1, M1T, K1) x 4, (S1, K1) x 3 = 24 B .. (S1, K1) x 3, (S2, K1) x 4, (S1, K1) x 3

Body cont.

11–19 A .. (S1, K1) x 3, (S1, K2) x 4, (S1, K1) x 3
       B .. (S1, K1) x 3, (S2, K1) x 4, (S1, K1) x 3

- Cut thread to 8". With sewing needle pick up stitches pocket style. Turn inside out. Form belly area when stuffing.

Arms

- Cast on 8 of #705
- DK rounds

Rounds	Side
1	A .. (K1, S1) x 4 B .. (K1, S1) x 4
2–11	Repeat as in round 1

Cut thread to 8". With sewing needle pick up stitches pocket style. Turn inside out. Stuff lightly, pull thread tight.

Legs

- Cast on 12 of #705
- DK rounds

Rounds	Side
1–4	A .. (K1, S1) x 6 B .. (K1, S1) x 6
5	A .. EDKS, K1, PSSR, S1, PSSR, (K1, S1) x 4 = 9 sts B .. (K1, S1) x 4, K1
6	A .. EDSK, (S1, K1) x 3, S1 = 8 sts B .. (K1, S1) x 4
7–13	A .. (K1, S1) x 4 B .. (K1, S1) x 4

- Cut thread to 8". With sewing needle pick up stitches pocket style. Turn inside out. Stuff lightly. Pull thread tight.

Ears

- Cast on 8 Stitches
- DK rounds in reverse
  (K1, bring thread forward, S1, bring thread to back)

Rounds	Side
1,2	A---(K1, S1) x 4 B---(K1, S1) x 4

- Cut thread to 8 inches, do not pick up stitches like a pocket, but go straight through row, over last loop and back again. Sew beginning thread down side and pull to form ear.

DK rounds in reverse:

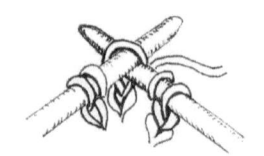

Put thread in back before knit stitch.

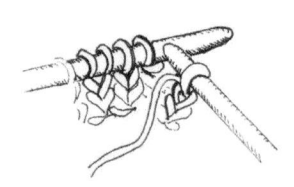

Bring thread forward before slipping the next stitch.

Finishing

Sew parts to body. **Eyes:** using DMC Black make a 3 loop french knot. **Nose:** 4 stitches.
Mouth: one verticle, one horizontal.

Lady Bug

Colors Red # 97   Black #240   DMC Black   DMC White

Body

- Cast on 8 of #240 black
- DK rounds

Rounds	Side
1	A .. K2, (S1, K1) x 3 B .. (S1, K1) x 4
2	A .. EIS, (S1, K1) x 4 = 9 sts B .. EIS, (S1, K1) x 4, S1 = 10 sts
3,4,5	A .. (K1, S1) x 5 B .. (K1, S1) x 5
6	A .. (K1, M1T, S1) x 5 = 15 sts B .. (K1, M1T, S2) x 5 = 20 sts
7,8	Change color to red #97 Do not cut black thread. A .. (K2, S2) x 10 B .. (K2, S2) x 10
9	Knit the stitch with #240 Black when marked with an * A .. K2, S2, *K1, K1, S2, K2, S2, K1, *K1, S2, K2, S2 B .. (K2, S2) x 10
10	Repeat as in round 7
11	A .. K1, *K1, (S2, K2) x 4, S2 B .. (K2, S2) x 10
12	A .. (K2, S2) x 4, *K1, K1, S2 B .. (K2, S2) x 10
13	A .. K2, S2, K1, *K1, (S2, K2) x 3, S2 B .. (K2, S2) x 10
14	A .. (K2, S2) x 3, *K1, K1, S2, K2, S2 B .. (K2, S2) x 10
15	A .. *K1, K1, (S2, K2) x 4, S2 B .. (K2, S2) x 10
16	A .. K2, S2, *K1, K1, (S2, K2) X2, S2, K1, *K1, S2 B .. (K2, S2) x 10
17	A .. (K2, S2) x 3, K1, *K1, S2, K2, S2 B .. (K2, S2) x 10
18,19	Repeat as in round 7

- Cut thread to 8". WIth sewing needle pick up stitches in pocket style, two knits, two slips at a time.

Finishing

Stuff ladybug and pull end closed, knot. Using black single strand DMC thread, sew around the bug where the black meets red in a gathering stitch. Pull to tighten to define the head. Knot. Make a line stitch down the center of the bug's back. Make two antennae with little knots on the end. DMC white single strand- sew a tiny stitch for each eye.

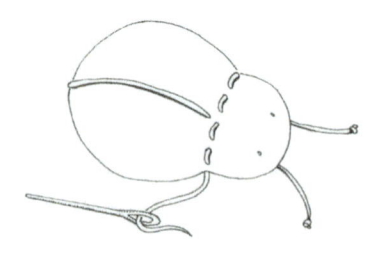

Donkey

Colors   #32 Grey   #229 Light Blue   #227 Medium Blue   #35 LightGrey   DMC Black

Body

- CO 14 of #229
- DK Rounds

Rounds	Sides
1-19	A .. (K1, S1) x 7 B .. (K1, S1) x 7
20	A .. (K1, S1) x 7 B .. EIK, (K1, S1 x 7) = 15 sts
21	A .. EDKS, (K1, S1) x 6, K1 =14 B .. EIS, (S1, K1) x 7 = 15
22	A .. EDSK, (S1, K1) x 6, S1 = 14 B .. EIK. (K1, S1) x 7) =15
23	Repeat round 21
24	Repeat round 22
25	Repeat round 21
26	Repeat round 22
27	A .. EDKS, (K1, S1) x 6, K1 = 14 B .. (S1,K1) x 7
28	A .. EDSK, (S1, K1) x 6 = 13 B .. (S1, K1) x 6, S1
29	A .. EDKS, (K1, S1) x5, K1 = 12 B .. (S1, K1) x 6
30	A .. EDSK, (S1, K1) x 5 = 11 B .. (S1, K1) x 5, S1
31	A .. EDKS, (K1, S1) X 4, K1 = 10 B .. (S1, K1) X 5
32, 33	A .. (S1, K1) x 5 B .. (S1, K1) x 5
34–36	Change color to #227 A .. (S1, K1) x 5 B .. (S1, K1) x 5
37, 38	Change to color #35 A .. (S1, K1) x 5 B .. (S1, K1) x 5
39	A .. EDSK. (S1, K1) x 4 = 9 B .. (S1, K1) x 4, S1
40	A .. EDKS, (K1, S1) x 3, K1 = 8 B .. (S1, K1) x 4
41	A .. (S1, K1) x 4 B .. (S1, K1) x 4

- Cut thread to 8". With sewing needle pick up stiches pocket style. Turn inside out. Stuff body and pull opening closed. Knot and hide thread.

Tail

- CO 2 of #229
- Tube Knitting
  Do 7 rows
- Cut thread to 8". With Sewing needle pick up stitches and pull shut.

Ears

- CO 2 of #229
- Single Rows

Rows

1 .. K1, M1, K1
2 .. Purl 3
3 .. K1, M1, K1, M1, K1 = 5 sts
4 .. Purl 5
5 .. K2, M1, K1, M1, K2 = 7 sts
6 .. Purl 7
7 .. Knit 7
8 .. Purl 7
9 .. Knit 7
10 .. Purl 7

- Cut thread to 8". With sewing needle pick up stitches straight through row. Sew beginning thread along back side to the base of the ear. Fold ear in half, length wise.

Hooves and Legs

- CO 8 of #32

- DK Rounds

Rounds	Sides
1-4	1 .. (K1, S1) x 4 2 .. (K1, S1) x 4
5-14	Change color to #229 Repeat as in round 1

- Cut thread to 8". With sewing needle pick up stitches pocket style. Turn inside out. Stuff legs, pull opening shut.

Finishing

Sew legs onto body. Sew ears in place. Sew on tail. **Fringe:** With #227 double thread a sewing needle. Make a fringe knot on the end of the tail with the double threaded needle. Make 5 fringe knots along the back of the neck for the mane. **Eye:** use Black DMC thread. Make a french knot with two wraps. **Mouth:** sew with two stitches side by side. **Nostrils:** one small stitch each.

Giraffe

Colors   Gold #203   Grey #32   DMC #938   DMC Black

Head and Body

- CO 18 of #203
- DK rounds

Rounds	Sides
1-7	A .. (K1, S1) x 9 B .. (K1, S1) x 9
8	A .. EDKS, (K1, S1) x 8 = 17 sts B .. (K1, S1) x 8, K1
9	A .. EDSK (S1, K1) x 7, S1 = 16 sts B .. (K1,S1) x 8
10	A .. EDKS, (K1, S1) x 7 = 15 sts B .. (K1, S1) x 7 , K1
11	A .. EDSK, (S1, K1) x 6, S1 = 14 sts B .. (K1, S1) x 7
12	A .. EDKS, (K1, S1) x 6 = 13 sts B .. (K1, S1) x 6, K1
13	A .. EDSK, (S1, K1) x 5, S1 = 12 sts B .. (K1, S1) x 6
14	A .. EDKS, (K1, S1) x 5 = 11 sts B .. (K1, S1) x 5, K1
15	A .. EDSK, (S1, K1) x 4, S1 = 10 sts B .. (K1, S1) x 5
16	A .. EDKS, (K1, S1) x 4 = 9 sts B .. (K1, S1) x 4, K1
17	A .. EDSK, (S1, K1) x 3, S1 = 8 sts B .. (K1, S1) x 4
17-36	A .. (K1, S1) x 4 B .. (K1, S1) x 4

- Cut thread to 8". With sewing needle pick up stitches pocket style. Turn inside out. Stuff. Gather end and knot. Using thread, take an angled stitch to bend head, knot and hide thread.

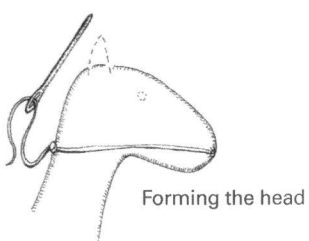

Forming the head

Front Legs

- CO 6 of #32
- DK rounds

Rounds	Side
1-4	A .. (K1, S1) x 3 B .. (K1, S1) x 3
5-23	Change to color #203 A .. (K1, S1) x 3 B .. (K1, S1) x 3

- Cut thread to 8". With sewing needle pick up stitches pocket style. Turn inside out. Pull thread to tighten end.

Back Legs

- CO 6 of #32
- DK rounds

Rounds	Side
1-4	A .. (K1, S1) x 3 B .. (K1, S1) x 3
5-18	Change to color #203 A .. (K1, S1) x 3 B .. (K1, S1) x 3
19	A .. EIK, (K1, S1) x 3 = 7 sts B .. (K1, S1) x 3, K1
20	A .. EIS, (S1, K1) x 3, S1 = 8 sts B .. (K1, S1) x 4
21-23	A .. (K1, S1) x 4 B .. (K1, S1) x 4

- Cut thread to 8". With sewing needle pick up stitches pocket style. Turn inside out. Put a slight amount of stuffing at top of leg where it widens. Do not pull tight, instead flatten the top of leg and sew it shut.

Flatten top of rear leg and sew shut

Ears

- CO 2
- Single Rows
  Row
  1 .. K1,M1,K1
  2 .. Purl 3
  3 .. Cast off
- Cut thread to 8". Sew beginning thread down to base of ear. Fold ear in half vertically and attach to head sewing both threads into it to secure the ear.

Tail

- CO 2
- Tube Knitting
  7 rows
- Cut thread to 8". With sewing needle pick up stitches and pull shut.

Finishing

Sew front legs to the base of the body. Flatten the back legs and sew on to the base of the body. Sew ears in place. Sew tail on. With a double threaded needle use DMC #938 to make tail fringe and mane. Sew spots on body with single thread #938 as shown in picture. **Eye:** use black, wrap 3 loops for french knot. **Nostrils** are mini stitches. **Mouth** is two stitches.

Dachshund

Colors #216 Dark Brown   DMC Black   DMC White

Body

- CO 12 of #216
- DK rounds

Rounds	Side
1-16	A .. (K1, S1) x 6 B .. (K1, S1) x 6
17	A .. EDKS, (K1, S1) x 5 = 11 sts B .. EDKS, (K1, S1) x 4, K1 = 10 sts
18	A .. (S1, K1) x 5 B .. (S1, K1) x 5
19	A .. S1, K1, S1, M1T, K1, S1, M1T, K1, M1T, S1, K1, M1T, S1, K1 = 14 sts B .. S1, K1, S2, K1, S3, K1, S2, K1, S1 K1
20	A .. S1, K1, S1 K2, S1, K3, S1, K2, S1, K1 B .. S1, K1, S2, K1, S3, K1 S2, K1, S1, K1
21	A .. S1, K1, S1, M1T, K2, S1, K3, S1, K2, M1T, S1, K1 = 16 sts B .. S1, (K1, S3) x 3, K1, S1, K1
22–29	A .. S1, K1, (S1, K3) x 3, S1, K1 B .. S1, (K1, S3) x 3, K1, S1, K1

- Cut thread to 8". With sewing needle pick up stitches pocket style. Turn inside out. Stuff the body, forming it so the torso remains thin and the head is larger. Pull opening shut, knot and hide thread.

Legs

- CO 6 of #216
- DK rounds

Rounds	Side
1-6	A .. (K1, S1) x 3 B .. (K1, S1) x 3

- Cut thread to 8". With sewing needle pick up stitches pocket style. Turn inside out. Stuff lightly. Pull shut.

Ears

- CO3 of #216
- Single rows

Row	
1 ..	Knit
2 ..	Purl
3 ..	Knit
4 ..	Purl
5 ..	Knit

- Cut thread to 8". With sewing needle pick up stitch loops straight through row, over one, and back through, gathering slightly. Stitch starting thread along back side of ear to base. Sew both threads into head to attach ear.

Tail

- CO 2 of #216
- Tube Knitting
  10 rows
- Cut thread to 8". With sewing needle pick up stitches and pull shut.

Finishing

Eye: use Black DMC to make a 3 loop french knot. Use White DMC to sew a loop around the black french knot. Catch on two ends.

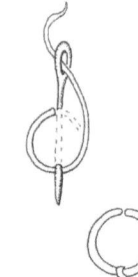

Eye Outline in white

Nose: use Black DMC making 7 vertical stitches as shown.
Mouth: two stitches as shown.

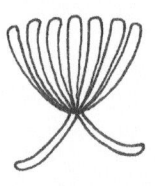

Nose and Mouth

Elephant

Colors # 19 Grey   DMC Black

Body and Trunk

- Starting with the trunk
  CO 3

  Rows
  1–10 .. Tube knitting on 3 stitches
  11 ..   Increase tube width .. M1, K3 = 4
  12–17 .. Continue tube knitting on 4 sts

- Single Rows

  Rows
  18 .. turn and purl across row
  19 .. K1, M1, K1, M1, K1, M1, K1 = 7
  20 .. P7
  21 .. S1, K1, M1, K1, M1, K1, M1, K1, M1, K1, S1 = 11
  22 .. P11
  23 .. S3, K1, M1, K1, M1, K1, M1, K1,M1, K1, S3 =15
  24 .. P15
  25 .. S5, K1, M1, K1, M1, K1, M1, K1, M1, K1, S5 = 19
  26 .. P19
  27 .. S6, K1, M1, K1, M1, K3, M1, K1, M1, K1, S6 = 23
  28 .. P23
  29 .. S6, K11, S6
  30 .. P23
  31 .. S7, K9, S7
  32 .. P23
  33 .. S5, K1, K2tog, K1, K2tog, K1, K2tog, K1, K2tog, K1, S5 = 19
  34 .. P19
  35 .. K2, K2tog, K3, K2tog, K1, K2 tog, K3, K2tog, K2 =15
  36 .. P15
  37 .. K1, M1, K3, M1, K3, M1, K1, M1, K3, M1, K3, M1, K1 = 21
  38 .. P21
  39 .. K4, M1, K4, M1, K5, M1, K4, M1, K4 = 25
  40 .. P25
  41–50 .. stockinette stitch on 25. (last row should be a purl)
  51 .. On knit side: K3, K2tog, K3, K2tog, K5, K2tog, K3, K2tog, K3 = 21
  52 .. P21
  53 .. K3, K2tog, K2, K2tog, K3, K2tog, K2, K2tog, K3 =17
  54 .. P17
  55 .. K2, K2tog, K2, K2tog, K1, K2tog, K2, K2tog, K2 =13
  56 .. Purl 13

- Cut thread to 8". With sewing needle pick up stitches. Leave thread to gather later. Fold with stockinette side in and trunk folded inside, with a sewing needle threaded with #19, stitch up the stomach, turn inside out. Use the rounded end of the toothpick tool to push out and shape the forehead area where the increase in stitches took place and stuff to allow this area to buldge a bit. Pull gathered stitches shut, knot and hide thread.

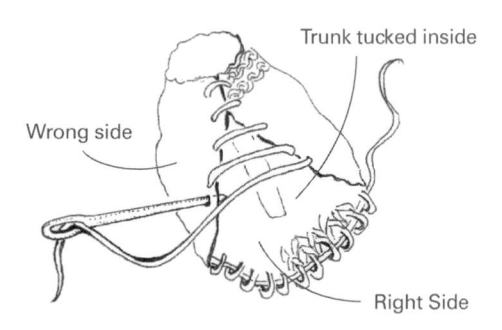

Trunk tucked inside
Wrong side
Right Side

Trunk folded inside. Stitch closed underside of elephant with purl side facing out.

Ears

- CO 5
- Single Rows

  Rows
  1 .. K1, M1,K3, M1, K1 = 7 sts
  2 .. P7
  3 .. K7
  4 .. P7
  5 .. K7
  6 .. P7
  7 .. K7

- Cut thread to 8". With sewing needle pick up stitches. Feed beginning thread through ear to base and sew into body also.

Tail

- CO 2
- Tube Knittting
  7 rows
- Cut thread to 8". With sewing needle pick up stitches and pull tube shut.

Legs

- CO 8
- DK Rounds

  Rounds   Side
  1–10   A .. (K1, S1) x 4
           B .. (K1, S1) x 4

- Cut thread to 8". With sewing needle pick up stitches pocket style. Turn inside out. Stuff lightly and pull shut.

Finishing

Sew legs in place. Sew ears on. **Eyes:** with Black DMC single thread do a french knot with 3 wraps. Sew on tail.

Octopus

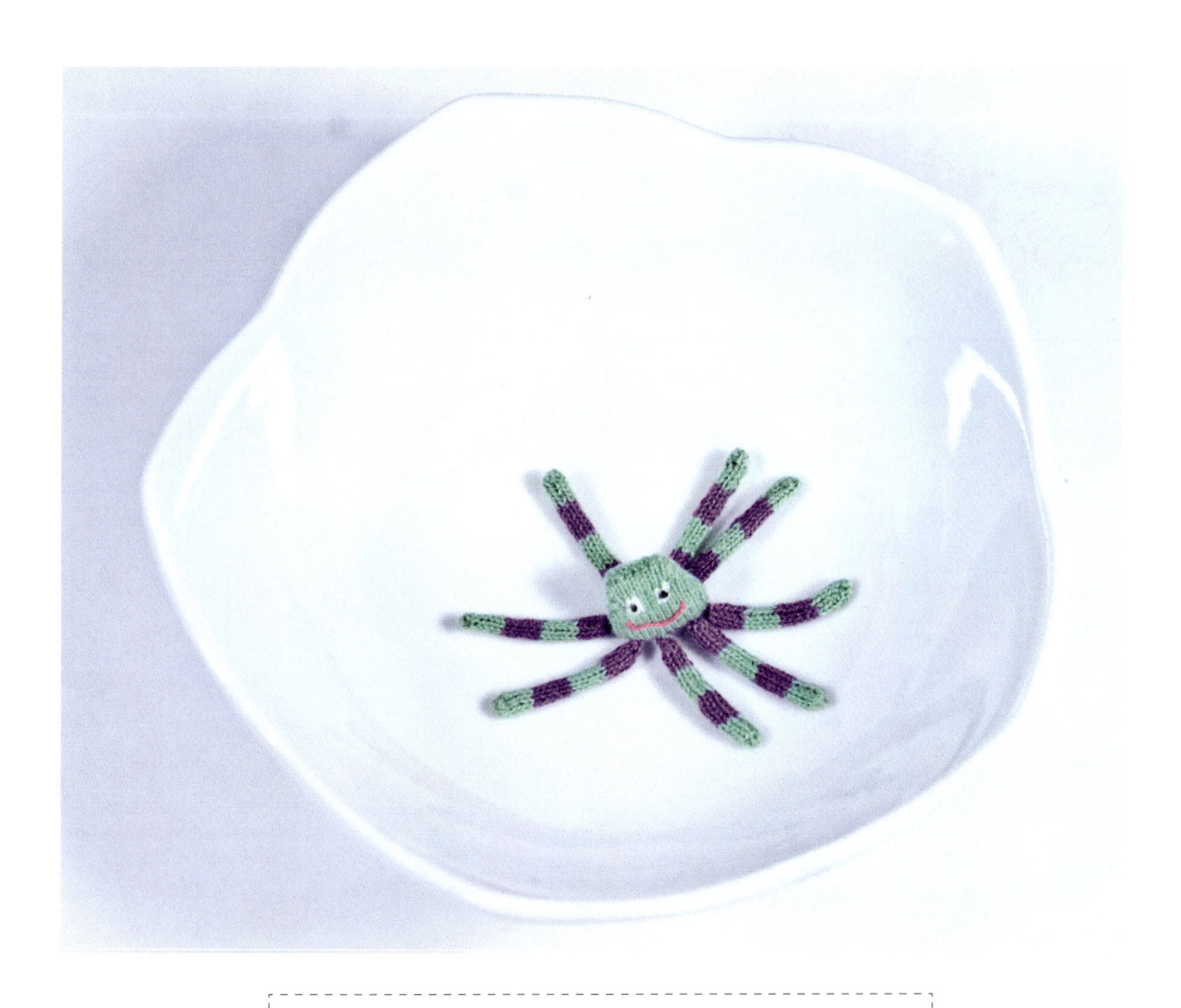

Colors # 224 Green #5 Purple White #37 Pink DMC Black

Body

- CO 16 of #224 Green
- DK rounds

Rounds	Sides
1-2	A ·· (K1, S1) x 8 B ·· (K1, S1) x 8
3	A ·· EIK, (K1, S1) x 8 = 17 sts B ·· EIK, (K1, S1) x 8, K1 = 18 sts
4	A ·· (S1, K1) x 9 B ·· (S1, K1) x 9
5	A ·· EIS, (S1, K1) x 9 = 19 sts B ·· EIS, (S1, K1) x 9, S1 = 20 sts
6	Each stitch for White eyes marked by * A ·· (K1, S1) x 2, (K1*, S1) x 2, (K1, S1) x 2, (K1*, S1) x 2, (K1, S1) x 2 B ·· (K1, S1) x 10
7	A ·· EIK, (K1, S1) x 2, (K1*, S1) x 2, (K1, S1) x2, (K1*, S1) x 2, (K1, S1) x 2 = 21 sts B ·· EIK, (K1, S1) x 10, K1 = 22 sts
8	A ·· S1, (K1, S1) x 2, (K1*, S1) x 2, (K1, S1) x 2 (K1*, S1) x 2, (K1, S1) x 2, K1 B ·· (S1, K1) x 11
9	A ·· EIS, (S1, K1) x 11 = 23 sts B ·· EIS, (S1, K1) x 11, S1 = 24 sts
10	A ·· (K1, S1) x 12 B ·· (K1, S1) x 12
11	A ·· EIK, (K1, S1) x 12 = 25 sts B ·· EIK, (K1, S1) x 12, K1 = 26 sts
12	A ·· (S1, K1) x 13 B ·· (S1, K1) x 13
13	A ·· EIS, (S1, K1) x 13 = 27 sts B ·· EIS, (S1, K1) x 13, S1 = 28 sts
14	A ·· (K1, S1) x 14 B ·· (K1, S1) x 14
15	A ·· EIK, (K1, S1) x 14 = 29 sts B ·· EIK, (K1, S1) x 14, K1 = 30 sts
16, 17	A ·· (S1, K1) x 15 B ·· (S1, K1) x 15
18, 19	Change to Purple #5 A ·· (S1, K1) x 15 B ·· (S1, K1) x 15
20	A ·· EDSK, (S1, K1) x 14 = 29 sts B ·· EDSK, (S1, K1) x 13, S1 = 28 sts
21	A ·· EDKS, (K1, S1) x 13 = 27 sts B ·· EDKS, (K1, S1) x 12, K1 = 26 sts
22	A ·· EDSK, (S1, K1) x 12 = 25 sts B ·· EDSK, (S1, K1) x 11, S1 = 24 sts
23	A ·· EDKS, (K1, S1) x 11 = 23 sts B ·· EDKS, (K1, S1) x 10, K1 = 22 sts
24	A ·· (S1, K1) x 11 B ·· (S1, K1) x 11

Cut thread to 8". With sewing needle pick up stitches pocket style. Turn inside out. Pull opening partially shut and set aside.

Arms

- CO 6 of Green #224
- DK rounds

Rounds	Side
1-6	A ·· (K1, S1) x 3 B ·· (K1, S1) x 3
7-12	Change to Purple #5, repeat as in round 1
13-18	Change to Green #224, repeat as in round 1
19-24	Change to Purple #5, repeat as in round 1

- Cut thread to 8". With sewing needle pick up stitches pocket style. Turn inside out. Pull thread to tighten end. Make eight arms.

Finishing

Stuff octopus head but leave the base open. Sew the eight arms evenly around the base, using 2 stitches to hold each arm. Knot the thread from two arms together as shown. Cut thread and tuck into stuffing hole. After all arms are secure, gather up the opening into an oval shape and sew the opening shut. Knot and hide the thread. For the face make the eyes with a 2 loop french knot using Black DMC. For the mouth use #37 Pink. Make a half circle for the smile and put the tiniest dab of glue in the center to hold it in place.

Dinosaur

Colors   # 100 Green   #506 Lime Green   DMC Black

Body

- CO 4 of #100
- DK Rounds

Rounds	Side
1–4	A .. (K1, S1) x 2 B .. (K1, S1) x 2
5	A .. EIK, (K1, S1) x 2 = 5 sts B .. EIK, (K1, S1) x 2, K1 = 6 sts
6–8	A .. (S1, K1) x 3 B .. (S1, K1) x 3
9	A .. EIS, (S1, K1) x 3 = 7 sts B .. EIS, (S1, K1) x 3, S1 = 8 sts
10–12	A .. (K1, S1) x 4 B .. (K1, S1) x 4
13	A .. EIK, (K1, S1) x 4 = 9 sts B .. EIK, (K1, S1) x 4, K1 = 10 sts
14–16	A .. (S1, K1) x 5 B .. (S1, K1) x 5
17	A .. EIS, (S1, K1) = 11 sts B .. EIS, (S1, K1) x 5, S1 = 12 sts
18, 19	A .. (K1, S1) x 6 B .. (K1, S1) x 6
20	A .. EIK, (K1, S1) x 6 = 13 sts B .. EIK, (K1, S1) x 6, K1 = 14 sts
21, 22	A .. (S1, K1) x 7 B .. (S1, K1) x 7
23	A .. EIS, (S1, K1) x 7 = 15 sts B .. EIS, (S1, K1) x 7, S1 = 16 sts
24	A .. (K1, S1) x 8 B .. (K1, S1) x 8
25	A .. EIK, (K1, S1) x 8 = 17 sts B .. EIK, (K1, S1) x 8, K1 = 18 sts
26	A .. (S1, K1) x 9 B .. (S1, K1) x 9
27	A .. EIS, (S1, K1) x 9 = 19 sts B .. EIS, (S1, K1) x 9, S1 = 20 sts
28	A .. (K1, S1) x 10 B .. (K1, S1) x 10
29	A .. EIK, (K1, S1) x 10 = 21 sts B .. EIK, (K1, S1) x 10, K1 = 22 sts
30	A .. (S1, K1) x 11 B .. (S1, K1) x 11
31	A .. EIS, (S1, K1) x 11 = 23 sts B .. EIS, (S1, K1) x 11, S1 = 24 sts
32	A .. EIK, (K1, S1) x 12 = 25 B .. EDKS, (K1, S1) x 11, K1 = 24 sts
33–35	A .. (S1, K1) x 12 B .. (S1, K1) x 12
36	A .. EIS, (S1, K1) x 12 = 25 sts B .. EDSK, (S1, K1) x 11, S1 = 24 sts
37–39	A .. (K1, S1) x 12 B .. (K1, S1) x 12
40	A .. EIK, (K1, S1) x 12 = 25 sts B .. EDKS, (K1, S1) x 11, K1 = 24 sts
41, 42	A .. (S1, K1) x 12 B .. (S1, K1) x 12
43	A .. EIS, (S1, K1) x 12 = 25 sts B .. EDKS, (K1, S1) x 11, S1 = 24 sts
44, 45	A .. (K1, S1) x 12 B .. (K1, S1) x 12
46	A .. (K1, S1) x 12 B .. EDKS, (K1, S1) x 11 = 23 sts
47	A .. (K1, S1) x 11, K1 B .. EDSK, (S1, K1) x 10, S1 = 22 sts
48	A .. (K1, S1) x 11 B .. EDKS, (K1, S1) x 10 = 21 sts
49	A .. (K1, S1) x 10, K1 B .. EDSK, (S1, K1) x 9, S1 = 20 sts
50	A .. (K1, S1) x 10 B .. EDKS, (K1, S1) x 9 = 19 sts
51	A .. (K1, S1) x 9, K1 B .. EDSK, (S1, K1) x 8, S1 = 18 sts
52	A .. (K1, S1) x 9 B .. EDKS, (K1, S1) x 8 = 17 sts

Body cont.

53	A .. (K1, S1) x 8, K1 B .. EDSK, (S1, K1) x 7, S1 = 16 sts
54	A .. (K1, S1) x 8 B .. EDKS, (K1, S1) x 7 = 15 sts
55	A .. (K1, S1) x 7, K1 B .. EDSK, (S1, K1) x 6, S1 = 14 sts
56	A .. (K1, S1) x 7 B .. EDKS, (K1, S1) x 6 = 13 sts
57	A .. EIK, (K1, S1) x 6, K1 = 14 sts B .. EDSK, (S1, K1) x 6 = 13 sts
58	A .. (S1, K1) x 6, S1 B .. EDKS, (K1, S1) x 5, K1 = 12 sts
59	A .. (S1, K1) x 6 B .. EDSK, (S1, K1) x 5 = 11 sts
60	A .. (S1, K1) x 5, S1 B .. EDKS, (K1, S1) x 4, K1 = 10 sts
61	A .. EIS, (S1, K1) x 5 = 11 sts B .. EDSK, (S1, K1) x 4, S1 = 10 sts
62–74	A .. (K1, S1) x 5 B .. (K1, S1) x 5

- Cut thread to 8". With sewing needle pick up stitches pocket style. Turn inside out. Stuff body, gather and knot.

Legs

- CO 6 of #100
- DK Rounds

Rounds	Side
1–6	A .. (K1, S1) x 3 B .. (K1, S1) x 3

- Cut thread to 8". With sewing needle pick up stitches pocket style. Turn inside out and pull shut.

Spikes

- CO 2 of # 506
- Single Rows

Rows

1 .. K2
2 .. K1, YO, K1
3 .. K1, YO, K2
4 .. K2, YO, K2
5 .. K3, YO, K2
6 .. K2, YO, K4
7 .. K5, YO, K2
8 .. Cast off 6, knit last stitch, leaving 2 on needle

- Repeat rows 1–8 three more times. On the third time, for row 8, cast off all stitches to complete. Cut thread to 8".

Finishing

Sew legs onto body. Sew spikes onto top of dinosaur with spikes aiming backward.
Eyes: using DMC black Make french knots with two loops.

Hippo

Colors #27 Lavender   #37 Hot Pink   DMC Black

Lower Mouth

- CO 14 of #27
- DK rounds

Rounds	Side
1	A .. (K1, S1) x 7 B .. (K1, S1) x 7
2	A .. EIK, (K1, S1) x 7 = 15 sts B .. EIK, (K1, S1) x 7, K1 = 16 sts
3-11	A .. (S1, K1) x 8 B .. (S1, K1) x 8

- Have two knitting needles on hand. With needle (1) pick up the first slip stitch knit-wise, and the next knit purl-wise. Now, with needle (2) pick up a slip purl-wise and with needle (1) pick up a knit purl-wise and repeat this across, so that the remaining slip stiches are on one needle, the knits on the other. This should leave you with 9 stitches on the back needle and 7 slip stitches on the other. Transfer the 9 stitches to a safety pin to hold them aside temporarily.

- Hold the needle with the seven stitches with the purl side facing you.

  Purl 7
  Turn .. Knit 7
  Turn .. Purl 7

- Cast off stitches. Cut thread to 8".

- Transfer the 9 stitches back to a knitting needle. Use the blunt end of the toothpick to push the cast off end into the pocket, along with the 8" thread. Set aside.

Upper Mouth

- Repeat rows 1–11 the same as for the lower mouth. Pick up the stitches onto two separate needles as before. Now remove the last slip stitch from the front needle and place it on the back with the knits. You should have 10 stitches on one needle and 6 on the other. Put the 10 stitches onto a safety pin. Hold the needle with the 6 remaining with the purl side facing you.

Upper Mouth cont.

- Purl 6
  Turn .. Knit 6
  Turn .. Purl 6

- Cast off stitches. Cut thread to 1". Transfer the remaining 10 stitches back on a knitting needle. Tuck the cast off end into pocket like the first mouth part.

Body

- Place the two mouth parts together with the pockets facing in, the 10 stiches on the back needle, the 9 on the front needle. With third needle pick up a stitch purl-wise from the needle in back, one off the needle in the front, one from the back, and so forth, until all the stitches are on = 19. To make this process go smoothly, make sure to push the needle up each time after removing a stitch and moving to the other needle. This will help to keep stitches from dropping off by accident. With 19 stitches on one needle you are ready for round one. To identify side A and B at this point, tie a knot in the starting thread that is hanging on the left to mark as side A.

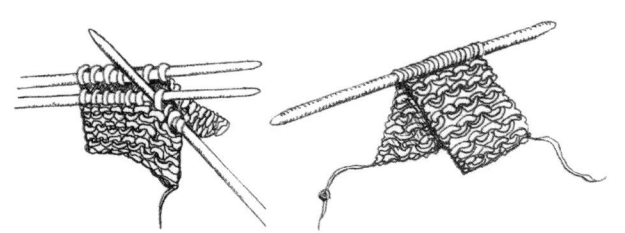

Put the two mouth parts together and pick up stitches alternately, starting with the back side.

The two mouths on one needle, Ready for Round 1 of Body. Put a knot on the left tail.

- For round one start with #27 on 19 stitches.

Rounds	Side
1	A .. (K1, S1) x 9, K1 B .. (S1, K1) x 9, S1
2	A .. (K1, S1) x 3, (K1, M1T, S1) x 4, (K1, S1) x 2, K1 = 23 sts B .. (S1, K1) x 3, (S2, K1) x 4, (S1, K1) x 2, S1

37

3-18	A ..	(K1, S1) x 3, (K2, S1) x 4, (K1, S1) x 2, K1
	B ..	(S1, K1) x 3, (S2, K1) x 4, (S1, K1) x 2, S1
19	A ..	EDKS, (K1, S1) x 2, (K2, S1) x 4, (K1, S1) x 2, K1 = 22 sts
	B ..	EDSK, (S1, K1) x 2, (S2, K1) x 4, (S1, K1) x 2 = 21 sts
20	A ..	S1, (K1, S1) x 2, (K2tog, S1) x 4, (K1, S1) x 2 = 17 sts
	B ..	(K1, S1) x 8, K1
21, 22	A ..	S1, (K1, S1) x 8
	B ..	(K1, S1) x 8, K1

- Cut thread to 8". With sewing needle pick up stitches pocket style. Before turning inside out, draw out the cast off mouth ends that were tucked in. With the 8" thread sew together the cast off ends along the sides and across the top.

Turn inside out. Stuff the upper and lower mouth lightly. Use your rounded end of the toothpick tool to form the forehead area and stuff carefully to accentuate it. Pull the opening closed. Knot and hide thread.

› Sewing the mouth flaps together

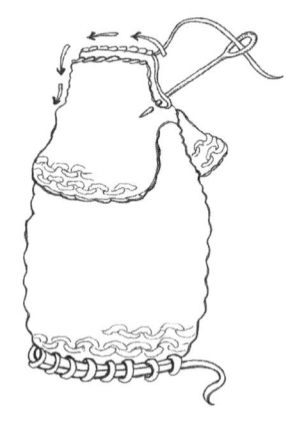

Tail

- CO 4
- Tube knitting
  4 rows
- Cut thread to 8". With sewing needle pick up stitches and pull tube shut.

Legs

- CO 8
- Double knit rounds
  Rounds   Side
  1-7   A .. (K1, S1) x 4
           B .. (K1, S1) x 4
- Cut thread to 8". With sewing needle pick up stitches pocket style. Turn inside out. Stuff. Pull closed.

Ears

- CO 4
- Single Rows
  Rows
  1 .. Knit
  2 .. Purl
- Cut thread to 8". Pick up stitches straight across with sewing needle. Over one and back through again. Sew casting thread down to base of ear.

Tongue

- Single Rows
- CO 3 of #37
  Rows
  1 .. K3
  2 .. P3
  3 .. K1, M1, K1, M1, K1
  4 .. P5
  5 .. K5
  6 .. Cast off on purl side.
- Cut thread to 8". Sew casting thread down side of mouth. Sew ends into base of mouth opening.

Finishing

Sew legs, ears, and tail onto body. Sew tongue into mouth. **Eyes:** Black DMC- 2 loops french knot
Nose: tiny stitch on each side.

Kittens

Colors for: White Cat   #727 Cream   DMC Pink   DMC Blue   DMC White
Siamese Cat   #727 Cream   #240 Black   DMC Blue   DMC White
Grey and White Cat   #727 Cream   #32 Grey   DMC Pink   DMC White

Head for Solid White Cat

- CO 18 of #727

- DK Rounds

Rounds	Side
1-4	A .. (K1, S1) x 9 B .. (K1, S1) x 9
5	A .. (K1, S1) x 4, M1T, K1, M1T, S1, (K1, S1) x 4 = 20 sts B .. (K1, S1) x 4, K1, S3, (K1, S1) x 4
6	A .. (K1, S1) x 3, M1T, K1, S1, K3, S1, K1, M1T, S1, (K1,S1) x 3 = 22 sts B .. (K1, S1) x 3, K1, S2, K1, S3, K1, S2, (K1, S1) x 3
7	A .. EDKS, (K1, S1) x 2, K2, M1T, S1, K3, S1, M1T, K2, S1, (K1, S1) x 3 = 23 sts B .. EDKS, (K1, S1) x 2,(K1, S3) x 3, (K1, S1) x 2, K1 = 22 sts
8	A .. EDSK, S1, K1, (S1, K3) x 3, (S1, K1) x 3 = 21 sts B .. EDSK, (S1, K1) x 2, (S3, K1) x 3, S1, K1, S1 = 20 sts
9-13	A .. (K1, S1) x 2, (K3, S1) x 3, (K1, S1) x 2 B .. (K1, S1) x 2, (K1, S3) x 3, (K1, S1) x 2

- Cut thread to 8". With sewing needle pick up stitches pocket style. Turn inside out. Using a needle threaded with # 727, sew the bases of ear closed so that stuffing won't reach them. Pull on the corners of the ears to make them pointed. Use the blunt end of the toothpick tool to push out the side with increases to form the face. Stuff. Pull opening shut. Knot.

Head for Siamese Cat

- CO 6 of #240 Black, tie on #727 and cast on 6, tie black thread to #727 and cast on 6 more = 18 sts

- DK Rounds

Note: Because #727 is in the center between the black stitches, carry the white thread around the underside of the knitting for each side A and B and entwine it with the black thread by bringing it under the black and over before knitting.

Rounds	Side
1-3	Knit the stitch with black when marked with an * A .. (K1*, S1) x 3, (K1, S1) x 3, (K1*, S1) x 3 B .. (K1*, S1) x 3, (K1, S1) x 3,(K1*, S1) x 3
4	A .. (K1*, S1) x2, (K1, S1) x 5, (K1*, S1) x 2 B .. (K1*, S1) x2, (K1, S1) x 5, (K1*, S1) x 2
5	A .. (K1*, S1) x 2, (K1, S1) x 2, M1T, K1, M1T, S1, (K1, S1) x 2, (K1*, S1) x 2 = 20 sts B .. (K1*, S1) x 2, (K1, S1) x 2, K1, S3, (K1, S1) x 2, (K1*, S1) x 2
6	A .. K1*, S1, (K1, S1) x 2, M1T, K1, S1, K3, S1, K1, M1T, (S1, K1) x 2, S1, K1*, S1 = 22 sts B .. K1*, S1, (K1, S1) x2, K1, S2, K1, S3, K1, S2, (K1, S1) x 2, K1*, S1
7	A .. EDKS, (K1, S1) x 2, K2, M1T, S1, K3, S1, M1T, K2, S1, (K1, S1) x 3 = 23 sts B .. EDKS, (K1, S1) x 2,(K1, S3) x 3, (K1, S1) x 2, K1 = 22 sts
8	A .. EDSK, S1, K1, (S1, K3) x 3, (S1, K1) x 3 = 21 sts B .. EDSK, (S1, K1) x 2, (S3, K1) x 3, S1, K1, S1 = 20
9-13	A .. (K1, S1) x 2, (K3, S1) x 3, (K1, S1) x 2 B .. (K1, S1) x 2, (K1, S3) x 3, (K1, S1) x 2

- Cut thread to 8". With sewing needle pick up stitches pocket style. Turn inside out. Using a needle threaded with black, sew the bases of ear closed so that stuffing won't reach them. Pull on the corners of the ears to make them pointed. Use the blunt end of the toothpick tool to push out the side with increases to form the face. Stuff. Pull opening shut. Knot.

Head for Grey and White Cat

- CO 18 of #32 Grey.
- DK Rounds

Rounds	Side
1-2	A .. (K1, S1) x 9 B .. (K1, S1) x 9
3	Use #727 for stitches marked with an * A .. (K1, S1) x 4, K1*, S1, (K1, S1) x 4 B .. (K1, S1) x 9
4	A .. (K1, S1) x 3, (K1*, S1) x 3, (K1, S1) x 3 B .. (K1, S1) x 9
5	A .. (K1, S1) x 3, K1*, S1, M1T*, K1*, M1T*, S1, K1*, S1, (K1, S1) x 3 = 20 sts B .. (K1, S1) x 4, K1, S3, (K1, S1) x 4
6	A .. (K1, S1) x 3, M1T*,K1*, S1, K3*, S1, K1*, M1T*, S1,(K1, S1) x 3 = 22 sts B .. (K1, S1) x 3, K1, S2, K1, S3, K1, S2, (K1, S1) x 3
7	A .. EDKS, (K1, S1) x 2, K2*, M1T*, S1, K3*, S1, M1T*, K2*, S1, (K1, S1) x 3 = 23 sts B .. EDKS, (K1, S1) x 2,(K1, S3) x 3, (K1, S1) x 2, K1 = 22 sts
8	A .. EDSK, S1, K1, S1, (K3*, S1) x 3, (K1, S1) x 2, K1 = 21 B .. EDSK, (S1, K1) x 2, (S3, K1) x 3, S1, K1, S1 = 20 sts
9-13	A .. (K1, S1) x 2, (K3*, S1) x 3, (K1,S1) x 2 B .. (K1, S1) x 2, (K1, S3) x 3, (K1, S1) x 2

- Cut thread to 8". With sewing needle pick up stitches pocket style. Turn inside out. Using a needle threaded with grey #32, sew the bases of ear closed so that stuffing won't reach them. Pull on the corners of the ears to make them pointed. Use the blunt end of the toothpick tool to push out the side with increases to form the face. Stuff. Pull opening shut. Knot.

Body for Solid White and Siamese Cat

- CO 16 of #727
- DK Rounds

Rounds	Side
1–17	A .. (K1, S1) x 8 B .. (K1, S1) x 8

- Cut thread to 8". With sewing needle pick up stitches pocket style. Turn inside out. Stuff. Pull opening closed. Knot. The gathered end of the body part is where the head will be attached.

Body for Grey and White Cat

- CO 16 of #32 Grey
- DK Rounds

Rounds	Side
1–12	A .. (K1, S1) x 8 B .. (K1, S1) x 8
13	Use #727 for stitches marked with an * A .. (K1, S1) x 3, (K1*, S1) x 2, (K1, S1) x 3 B .. (K1, S1) x 8
14	A .. (K1, S1) x 2, (K1*, S1) x 4, (K1, S1) x 2 B .. (K1, S1) x 8
15-17	A .. K1, S1, (K1*, S1) x 6, K1, S1 B .. (K1, S1) x 8

- Cut thread to 8". With sewing needle pick up stitches pocket style. Turn inside out. Stuff. Pull opening closed. Knot. The gathered end of the body part is where the head will be attached.

41

Legs for Solid White Cat

- CO 6 of #727

- DK Rounds

Rounds	Side
1–9	A .. (K1, S1) x 3
	B .. (K1, S1) x 3

- Cut thread to 8". With sewing needle pick up stitches pocket style. Turn inside out. Stuff Lightly. Pull thread to shut.

Legs for Grey and White Cat

- CO 6 of #727

- DK Rounds

Rounds	Side
1–4	A .. (K1, S1) x 3
	B .. (K1, S1) x 3
5-9	Change to #32 Grey
	A .. (K1, S1) x 3
	B .. (K1, S1) x 3

- Cut thread to 8". With sewing needle pick up stitches pocket style. Stuff lightly. Turn inside out. Pull thread to shut.

Legs for Siamese Cat

- CO 6 of Black

- DK Rounds

Rounds	Side
1–4	A .. (K1, S1) x 3
	B .. (K1, S1) x 3
5-9	Change to #727 White
	A .. (K1, S1) x 3
	B .. (K1, S1) x 3

- Cut thread to 8". With sewing needle pick up stitches pocket style. Turn inside out. Stuff lightly. Pull thread to shut.

Rear Legs for Siamese Cat

- CO 4 of Black

- Tube Knitting

    Rows
    1 .. K4
    2 .. K1, M1, K2, M1, K1 = 6 sts
    3 .. K6
    4 .. K6

- Single Rows

    Change color to #727

    Rows
    5 .. Turn and purl 6
    6 .. K2, M1, K1, M1, K1, M1, K2 = 9sts
    7 .. P9
    8 .. K3, (M1, K1) x 3, M1, K3 = 13 sts
    9 .. P13
    10 .. K13
    11 .. P13
    12 .. K2, K2tog, K2tog, K1, K2tog, K2tog, K2 = 9 sts
    13 .. P9

- Cut thread to 8". With sewing needle pick up stitches and gather to close. Fold in half to form leg. Sew halves together.

Tail for White or Siamese Cat

- CO 3 of #727 for white cat

    CO 3 of Black for Siamese cat

- Tube Knitting
    14 rows

- Cut thread to 8". With sewing needle pick up stitches and pull tube shut.

Tail for Grey and White Cat

- CO 3 of #727 White

- Tube Knitting
    4 rows

    Change to #32 Grey

    10 rows

- Cut thread to 8". With sewing needle pick up stitches and pull tube shut.

Finishing

Sew head, legs and tail to body. For the eyes make a three loop french knot with DMC thread. Use three stitches of a DMC color for the nose. One tiny horizontal stitch for the mouth. Use a strand of DMC white for the whiskers. Enter one cheek with the thread, take a stitch up to just behind the ear and back out the other cheek to secure. With a needle separate the fibers of the thread. Use a touch of oil to define the whiskers.

Spotted Dog

Colors   #727 Cream   # 213 Brown   Black DMC   White DMC

Body

- Cast on 20 of #727 Cream
- DK rounds

The body has two brown spots.
Use brown # 213 for the stitches noted by an *. Pick up colors as they are called for and let the thread of the other color follow along loosely on the back side.

Rounds	Side
1–3	A ·· (K1, S1) x 10 B ·· (K1, S1) x 10
4	A ·· (K1, S1) x 3, (*K1, S1) x 2, (K1, S1) x 5 B ·· (K1, S1) x 10
5–7	A ·· (K1, S1) x 2, (*K1, S1) x 5, (K1, S1) x 3 B ·· (K1, S1) x 10
8	A ·· (K1, S1) x 3, (*K1, S1) x 3, (K1, S1) x 4 B ·· (K1,S1) x 10
9	A ·· (K1, S1) x 4 , (*K1, S1) x 2, (K1, S1) X 4 B ·· (K1, S1) x 10
10,11	Repeat as in round 1
12	A ·· (K1, S1) x 5, (*K1, S1) x 2, (K1, S1) x 3 B ·· (K1, S1) x 10
13.	A ·· (K1, S1) x 5, (*K1, S1) x 3, (K1, S1) x 2 B ·· (K1, S1) x 10
14	A ·· (K1, S1) x 5, (*K1, S1) x 4, K1, S1 B ·· (K1, S1) x 10
15	A ·· (K1, S1) x 6, (*K1, S1) x 2, (K1, S1) x 2 B ·· (K1, S1) x 10
16,17	Repeat as in round 1

- Tie the two ends of the brown thread together leaving it loose for stretching when stuffed. Cut cream thread to 8" and pick up stitches pocket style with sewing needle. Turn inside out. Stuff body. Gather end shut and knot. The head will be attached at this end.

Legs

- CO 6 of #727
- DK rounds

Rounds	Side
1–6	A ·· (K1, S1) x 3 B ·· (K1, S1) x 3

- Cut thread to 8". With sewing needle pick up stitches pocket style. Turn inside out. Stuff leg lightly.

Head

- Cast on 10 of cream #727
Use #213 brown for stitches marked with a *.
- DK rounds

Rounds	Side
1,2	A ·· (K1, S1) x 5 B ·· (K1, S1) x 5
3	A ·· EIK, (K1, S1) x 5 = 11 sts B ·· EIK, (K1, S1) x 5, K1 = 12 sts
4	A ·· (S1, K1) x 6 B ·· (S1, K1) x 6
5	A ·· S1, K1, (S1, K1, M1T) x 4, S1, K1= 16 sts B ·· S1, K1, (S2, K1) X 4, S1, K1
6	A ·· S1, K1, (S1, K2) x 2, S1, K1, *K1, S1, *K1, K1, S1, K1 B ·· S1, K1, (S2, K1) x 4, S1, K1
7,8	A ·· S1, K1, (S1, K2) x 2, S1, (*K2, S1) x 2, K1 B ·· S1, K1, (S2, K1) x 4, S1, K1
9	A ·· S1, K1, S1, M1T, (K2, S1) X 2, K1, *K1, S1,*K1, K1, M1T, S1, K1 = 18 sts B ·· S1, K1, S3, K1, (S2, K1) x 2, S3, K1, S1, K1
10–13	A ·· S1,K1, S1, K3, (S1, K2) x 2, S1, K3, S1, K1 B ·· S1, K1, S3, K1, (S2, K1) x 2, S3, K1, S1, K1

- Cut thread to 8". With sewing needle pick up stitches pocket style. Turn inside out. Stuff head and pull thread to close. Knot, hide thread.

Ears

- CO 3 of #213

    Rows
    1. K1,M1,K1,M1,K1
    2. Purl 5
    3. Knit
    4. Purl
    5. Knit
    6. Purl
    7. Knit
    8. Purl

- Cut thread to 8". With sewing needle go straight through all stitches, over one and back through to beginning.

Tail

- CO 3 of #213
- Tube Knitting
    4 rows

    Change to #727
    Do not knot threads together, but carry both colors up inside tubing.

    5 rows
- Cut thread to 8". With sewing needle gather stitches and pull shut.

Finishing

Sew legs, ears, and tail onto body. For the eyes make a double french knot in black DMC. On brown side do a circle of white around eye. Use black DMC for the nose.

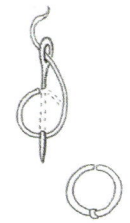

White stitching around eye

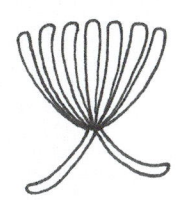

Nose and mouth

Turtle

Colors Olive #237   Lime Green #506   Dark Green #238

Turtle Shell

- CO 12 of Olive green #237
- DK Rounds

Do not cut threads when changing colors on rounds.

Rounds	Side
1	A .. (K1, S1) x 6 B .. (K1, S1) x 6
2	A .. EIK, (K1, S1) x 6 = 13 sts B .. EIK, (K1, S1) x 6, K1 = 14 sts
3	A .. EIS, (S1, K1) x 7 = 15 sts B .. EIS, (S1, K1) x 7, S1 = 16 sts
4	Change to Lime Green #506 A .. EIK, (K1, S1) x 8 = 17 sts B .. EIK, (K1, S1) x 8, K1 = 18 sts
5	Change to #237 A .. EIS, (S1, K1) x 9 = 19 sts B .. EIS, (S1, K1) x 9, S1 = 20 sts
6	A .. (K1, S1) x 10 B .. (K1, S1) x 10
7	A .. EIK, (K1, S1) x 10 = 21 sts B .. EIK, (K1, S1) x 10, K1 = 22 sts
8	Change to #506 A .. (S1, K1) x 11 B .. (S1, K1) x 11
9	Change to #237 A .. EIS, (S1, K1) x 11 = 23 B .. EIS, (S1, K1) x 11, S1 = 24 sts
10, 11, 12	A .. (K1, S1) x 12 B .. (K1, S1) x 12
13	Change to #506 A .. EDKS, (K1, S1) x 11 = 23 sts B .. EDKS, (K1, S1) x 10, K1 = 22 sts
14	Change to #237 A .. (S1, K1) x 11 B .. (S1, K1) x 11
15	A .. EDSK, (S1, K1) x 10 = 21 sts B .. EDSK, (S1, K1) x 9, S1 = 20 sts
16	A .. (K1, S1) x 10 B .. (K1, S1) x 10
17	Change to #506 A .. EDKS, (K1, S1) x 9 = 19 sts B .. EDKS, (K1, S1) x 8, K1 = 18 sts
18	Change to #237 A .. EDSK, (S1, K1) x 8 = 17 sts B .. EDSK, (S1, K1) x 7, S1 = 16 sts
19	A .. EDKS, (K1, S1) x 7 = 15 sts B .. EDKS, (K1, S1) x 6, K1 = 14 sts
20	A .. EDSK, (S1, K1) x 6 = 13 sts B .. EDSK, (S1, K1) x 5, S1 = 12 sts
21	A .. (K1, S1) x 6 B .. (K1, S1) x 6

- Cut thread to 8". With sewing needle pick up stitches pocket style. Turn inside out. Stuff lightly. Pull closed. Knot.

Head

- CO 8 of Dark Green #238
- DK Rounds

Rounds	Side
1–10	A .. (K1, S1) x 4 B .. (K1, S1) x 4

- Cut thread to 8". With sewing needle pick up stitches pocket style. Turn inside out. Stuff lightly. Pull opening shut.

Feet

- CO 6 of Dark Green #238
- DK Rounds

Rounds	Side
1–8	A .. (K1, S1) x 3 B .. (K1, S1) x 3

- Cut thread to 8". Pick up stitches pocket style. Turn inside out. Pull opening shut.

Tail

- CO 2 of Dark Green #238
- Tube knitting
  7 rows
- Cut thread to 8". With sewing needle pick up stitches and pull tube shut.

Turtle Shell Edging

- Start with a 30" piece of #506 and do an embroidered chain stitch all the way around the rim of the body. It takes about 10 chain stitches for each half, 20 all the way around.

Embroidered Chain Stitch: Make a loop with the thread and bring needle through start hole back up through to catch the loop.

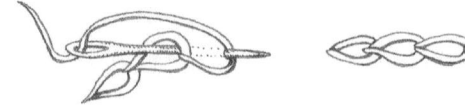

- With the remainder of #506 thread, use a crochet hook to create a decorative edging. Put hook through 1st embroidered chain and make 3 chain stitches, Slip stich into next embroidered chain. Repeat all the way around up to the last embroidered chain. Chain 3, pull thread through loop and tighten. With sewing needle, stitch into last chain, and hide thread.

Crochet Chain Stitch: Wrap thread around hook and pull through loop to make a chain stitch.

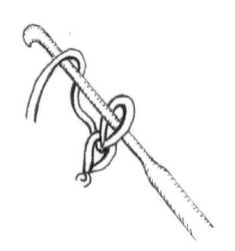

Crochet Slip stitch-After chain 3, enter next embroidered chain with hook, wrap thread around hook, and slip through both loops.

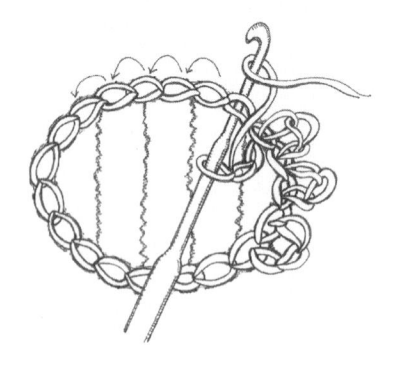

Finishing

Sew legs head and tail on to body underneath the decorative edging. Eyes: 1 small stitch for each eye of #506.

Panda Pair

Colors #727 Cream #240 Black DMC Black DMC #797 DMC #894

Body and Head

- CO 12 of #727 Cream
- DK rounds

Rounds	Side
1-12	A .. (K1, S1) x 6 B .. (K1, S1) x 6
13	A .. EIK, (K1, S1) x 6 = 13 B .. EIK, (K1, S1) x 6, K1 = 14
14-17	A .. (S1, K1) x 7 B .. (S1, K1) x 7

- Cut thread to 8". With sewing needle pick up stitches pocket style. Turn inside out. Stuff and pull the opening shut and knot. This is the top of the Panda bear. Poke the needle downward and exit at the spot just below round 13 where the stitches were increased. With small stitches gather round and tighten to make the neck. Knot and hide thread.

Arms

- CO 6 of #240 Black
- DK rounds

Rounds	Side
1-6	A .. (K1, S1) x 3 B .. (K1, S1) x 3

- Cut thread to 8". With sewing needle pick up stitches pocket style. Turn inside out. Pull opening shut.

Legs

- CO 6 of #240 Black
- DK rounds

Rounds	Side
1-9	A .. (K1, S1) x 3 B .. (K1, S1) x 3

- Cut thread to 8". With sewing needle pick up stitches pocket style. Turn inside out. Pull opening shut.

Ears

- CO 4 of #240 Black
- Single Rows
  1 .. K4
  2 .. P4

- Cut thread to 8". With sewing needle pick up stitches and pull tight. Sew beginning thread down side of ear.

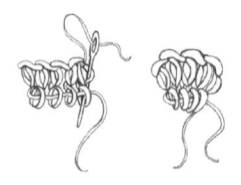

Finishing

Sew arms onto the side of the body just below the neckline. Sew the legs onto the base of the body. Sew the ears onto the top of the head. Using Black DMC thread make three stitches for each eye. Make around five stitches for the nose, and a vertical and horizontal stitch for the mouth.

Boy's Overalls

- CO 11 of DMC single thread #797 Blue, leaving an 8" thread at start

- Single Rows

  Rows
  1. K11
  2. K11
  3. P11
  4. K11
  5. P11
     This forms one trouser leg. Set aside and make one more. Line legs up on one needle with knit side toward front.
  6. Knit across all 22 sts.
  7. P22
  8. K22
  9. P22
  10. K22
  11. P22
  12. Cast off 8 sts, Knit 5 to equal 6 sts on right needle. Cast off remaining 8 sts. Cut thread to 14".
  13. With Sewing needle, stitch the thread back to the 6 remaining stitches. Pearl across the 6 sts.
  14. K6
  15. P6
  16. K6
  17. Cast off all 6 sts. Do not cut thread.

- **Finishing**

  Sew up the seams of the legs and back on the wrong side and turn inside out. Fit onto Panda boy and sew cross-over straps from the front bib to back. Knot and hide threads.

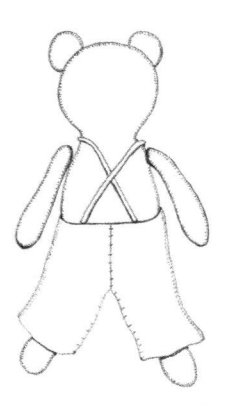

Girl's Dress

- CO 36 of DMC single thread #894 Pink, leaving an 8" thread at start

- Single Rows

  Rows
  1. K36
  2. P36
  3. K36
  4. P36
  5. K36
  6. P36
  7. P2, K2 across
  8. P2, K2 across
  9. P2tog, K2 across = 27 sts
  10. P2tog, K1 across = 18 sts
  11. Cast off 6 sts, Knit the next 5 to equal 6 stitches on the right needle. Cast off the remaining 6 sts. Cut thread to 14".
  12. With sewing needle, stitch thread back to the 6 remaining stitches. Pearl across the 6 sts.
  13. K6
  14. P6
  15. K6
  16. Cast off all 6 sts. Do not cut thread.

- **Finishing**

  Sew up the back seam of the skirt. Fit onto Panda girl and sew cross-over straps from the front bib to back. Knot and hide threads.

Kangaroo

Color #6 Tan, DMC Black

Body

- CO 4 of #6
- DK Rounds

Rounds	Side
1–4	A .. (K1, S1) x 2 = 4 sts B .. (K1, S1) x 2
5	A .. EIK, (K1, S1) x 2 = 5 sts B .. EIK, (K1, S1) x 2, K1 = 6 sts
6–10	A .. (S1, K1) x 3 = 6 sts B .. (S1, K1) x 3 = 6 sts
11	A .. EIS, (S1, K1) x 3 = 7 sts B .. EIS, (S1, K1) x 3, S1 = 8 sts
12–15	A .. (K1, S1) x 4 B .. (K1, S1) x 4
16	A .. EIK, (K1, S1) x 4 = 9 sts B .. EIK (K1, S1) x 4, K1 = 10 sts
17–22	A .. (S1, K1) x 5 = 10 sts B .. (S1, K1) x 5 = 10 sts
23	A .. EIS, Put stitch back on left needle .. Cast on one more stitch on left needle. K2, (S1, K1) x 5 = 12 sts B .. EIS, Put stitch back on left needle .. Cast on one more stitch on left needle. K2, (S1, K1) x 6 = 14 sts
24	A .. (S1, K1) x 7 = 14 sts B .. (S1, K1) x 7 = 14 sts
25	A .. (S1, MIT, K1) x 7 = 21 B .. (S2, K1) x 7 = 21 sts
26	A .. (S1, K2) x 7 = 21 B .. (S2, K1) x 7
27	A .. EIS, (S1, K2) x 7 = 22 sts B .. EIS, (S2, K1) X 7, S1 = 23 sts
28	A .. EIK, K1, (S1, K2) x 7, S1 = 24 sts B .. EIK, K1, (S2, K1) x 7, S1, K1 = 25 sts
29	A .. EIS, S1, K1, (S1, K2) x 7, S1, K1 = 26 sts B .. EIS, S1, K1, (S2, K1) x 7, S1, S1 = 27 sts
30	A .. K1, S1, K1, (S1, K2) x 7, S1, K1, S1 B .. K1, S1, K1, (S2, K1) x 7, S1, K1, S1
31	A .. (K1, S1) x 2, K2, S1, K1*- (marker on this stitch) With a sewing needle threaded with black DMC, slide through the loop of this knit and then make a loose knot. Cut and tuck into the interior of the knitted body. K1, (S1, K2) x 3, S1, K1* (marker on this stitch), K1, S1, K2, S1, K1, S1. B .. K1, S1, K1, (S2, K1) x 7, S1, K1, S1
32–34	Repeat as in round 30.
35	A .. (K1, S1) x 2, K2tog, (S1, K2) x 5, S1, K2tog, S1, K1, S1 = 25 sts B .. (K1, S1) x 2, K1, (S2, K1) x 5, S1, (K1, S1) x 2, = 25
36	A .. (K1, S1) x 2, K1, (S1, K2) x 5, S1, (K1, S1) x 2 B .. (K1, S1) x 2, K1, (S2, K1) x 5, S1, (K1, S1) x 2, = 25
37.	A .. (K1, S1) x 3, K2tog, (S1, K2) x 3, S1, K2tog, S1, (K1, S1) x 2 = 23sts B .. (K1, S1) x 3, K1, (S2,K1) x 3, S1, (K1, S1) x 3 =23
38	A .. (K1, S1) x 3, K1, (S1, K2) x 3, S1, (K1, S1) x 3 = 23 B .. (K1, S1) x 3, K1, (S2, K1) x 3, S1, (K1, S1) x 3 = 23
39	A .. (K1, S1) x 4, K2tog, S1, K2, S1, K2tog, S1, (K1, S1) x 3 = 21sts B .. (K1, S1) x 4, K1, S2, (K1, S1) x 5 = 21
40	A .. (K1, S1) x 5, K2tog, S1, (K1, S1) x 4 = 20 B .. (K1, S1) x 10 = 20
41	A .. (K1, S1) x 10 B .. (K1, S1) x 10
42	A .. EDKS, (K1, S1) x 9 = 19 sts B .. EDKS, (K1, S1) x 8, K1 = 18 sts
42	A .. (S1, K1) x 9 B .. (S1, K1) x 9
43	A .. EDSK, (S1, K1) x 8 = 17 sts B .. EDSK, (S1, K1) x 7, S1 = 16 sts
44	A .. (K1, S1) X 8 = 16 B .. (K1, S1) X 8
45	A .. EDKS, (K1, S1) X 7 = 15sts B .. EDKS, (K1, S1) x 6, K1 = 14sts
46–48	A .. (S1, K1) x 7 = 14 B .. (S1, K1) x 7 = 14
49	A .. EDSK, (S1, K1) x 6 = 13 sts B .. EDSK, (S1, K1) x 5, S1 = 12 sts

50,51 A .. (K1, S1) x 6 = 12
       B .. (K1, S1) x 6 = 12

Cut thread to 8". Pick up stitches pocket style. Turn inside out and add pouch in between marked areas.

Pouch

- Hold knitting needle across the area between the markers and with a sewing needle stitch 8 loops to body around the knitting needle arranging threads as shown in illustration. The feed thread on the card will be on the right side.

- **Single Rows**
  1 .. Knit 8
  2 .. Purl 8
  3 .. K2, M1, K2, M1, K2, M1, K2 = 11 sts
  4 .. Purl 11
  5 .. Knit 11
  6 .. P2, M1, P7, M1, P2 = 13 sts
  7 .. Knit 13
  8 .. Purl 13
  9 .. Knit 13
  10 .. Cast off.

- Cut thread to 8". Sew sides of pocket to body. knot, and hide threads. Stuff body, forming the tummy area and pull opening shut and knot. Hide thread.

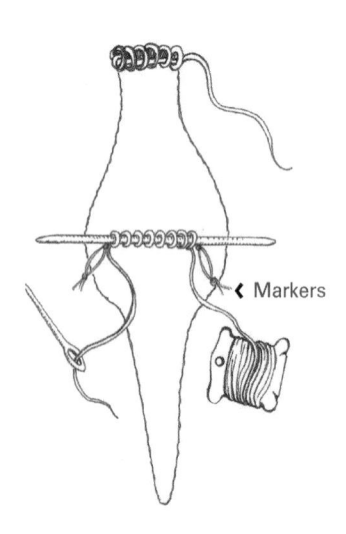

Legs

- CO6 #6
- Tube Knitting
  Rows 1-11
- Single Rows
  Rows
  12 .. Turn and purl 6
  13 .. (K1, M1) x 5, K1 = 11 sts
  14 .. Purl 11
  15 .. S2, (K1, M1) x 7, S2 = 18 sts
  16 .. purl 18
  17 .. S2, M1, (K2, M1) x 7, S2 = 26
  18 .. Purl 26
  19 .. S6, K 14, S6
  20 .. Purl 26
  21 .. S6, K14, S6
  22 .. Purl 26

- Cut thread to 8". With sewing needle pick up stitches. Pull tight and let the knitting fold vertically to form the knee shape. Form as shown in illustration.

Arms

- CO4 #6
- DK Rounds

Rounds	Side
1–3	A .. (K1, S1) x 2 B .. (K1, S1) x 2
4	A .. EIK, (K1, S1) x 2 = 5 sts B .. EIK, (K1, S1) x 2, K1 = 6 sts
5,6.	A .. (S1, K1) x 3 B .. (S1, K1) x 3
7	A .. EIS, (S1, K1) x 3 = 7 sts B .. EIS, (S1, K1) x 3, S1 = 8 sts
8–10	A .. (K1, S1) x 4 B .. (K1, S1) x 4

- Cut thread to 8". With sewing needle pick up stitches pocket style and turn arm inside out, pull shut.

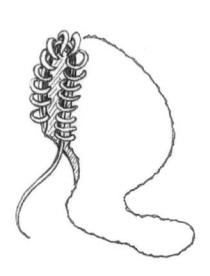

‹ Markers

Ears

- CO2 of #6

  Rows
  1 ·· K1, M1, K1
  2 ·· P3
  3 ·· K1, M1, K1, M1, K1 = 5 sts
  4 ·· P5
  5 ·· K2, M1, K1, M1, K2 = 7 sts
  6 ·· P7
  7 ·· K7
  8 ·· P7

- With sewing needle gather up stitches, pull and fold ear in half vertically.

Head

- CO 6 of #6

Rounds	Side
1–4	A ·· (K1, S1) x 3 B ·· (K1, S1) x 3
5	A ·· EIK, (K1, S1) x 3 = 7 sts B ·· EIK, (K1, S1) x 3, K1 = 8 sts
6	A ·· (S1, K1) x 4 B ·· (S1, K1) x 4
7	A ·· EIS, (S1, K1) x 4 = 9 sts B ·· EIS, (S1, K1) x 4, S1 = 10 sts
8	A ·· EIK, (K1, S1) x 5 = 11 sts B ·· EIK, (K1, S1) x 5, K1 = 12 sts
9,10	A ·· (S1, K1) x 6 B ·· (S1, K1) x 6
11	A ·· EIS, (S1, K1) x 6 = 13 sts B ·· EIS, (S1, K1) x 6, S1 = 14 sts
12–15	A ·· (K1, S1) x 7 B ·· (K1, S1) x 7

- Cut thread to 8". With sewing needle pick up stitches pocket style, turn inside out, stuff and pull shut. Knot.

Finishing Mama Kangaroo

Sew ears to head, head to neck. Sew arms and legs on. Use Black DMC for eyes- making two stitches to form a v shape for each. About 5 stitches for nose. One straight down and across for the mouth. Two stitches for claws on the paws and feet.

Baby Kangaroo

Head and Body

- CO 6 of #6

Rounds	Side
1–7.	A ·· (K1, S1) x 3 B ·· (K1, S1) x 3
8	A ·· EIK, (K1, S1) x 3 = 7 sts B ·· EIK, (K1, S1) x 3, K1 = 8 sts
9–12	A ·· (S1, K1) x 4 B ·· (S1, K1) x 4
13	A ·· EIS, (S1, K1) x 4 = 9 sts B ·· EIS, (S1, K1) x 4, S1 = 10 sts
14	A ·· (K1, S1) x 5 = 10 B ·· (K1, S1) x 5

- Cut thread to 8". With sewing needle pick up stitches pocket style. Turn inside out. Stuff and pull. Knot. Sew thread through the inside back up to the 7th round and pull and knot to form a bend to shape the head. sew a loop around to tighten for a neck. (See giraffe head Illustration for reference.)

Arms

- CO4 of #6

Rounds	Side
1–3	A ·· (K1, S1) x 2 B ·· (K1, S1) x 2

- Cut thread to 8". With sewing needle pick up stitches pocket style. Turn inside out. Pull shut.

Ears

- CO 2 of #6

  Rows
  1 ·· K1, M1, K1
  2 ·· P3
  3 ·· K3

- Cut thread to 8". With sewing needle gather up the three stitches.

Finishing Baby Kangaroo

Sew Ears to head and arms to body. With Black DMC make a small stitch for each eye. Two small stitches for the nose. Small stitch for mouth. Tuck baby into Mom's pouch.

Glossary of Terms

CO – Cast on

Cast Off – Knit two stitches, pass right stitch over left stitch and off needle. Repeat across row.

DK Round – One round has a side A and a Side B. The starting thread of the cast-on stitches is on the left for side A, the right for Side B.

Double thread – Thread sewing needle so that a thread hangs on each side of the needle eye

EDKS – Edge Decrease: Knit, Slip, Pass Knit over Slip and off needle

EDSK – Edge Decrease: Slip, Knit, Pass Slip over Knit and off needle

EIK – Edge Increase on knit. Stitch added to base of Knit stitch at beginning of row.

EIS – Edge Increase on slip. Stitch added to base of Slip stitch at beginning of row.

Feed thread – The thread that is used for knitting

Hide thread – Sewing the thread back into the form to hide it rather than knotting.

K – Knit

K2tog – Knit two together.

Knit-wise – When picking up a stitch to the right needle enter it as if knitting

M1 – Make 1 - An increase by making a loop over the right needle

M1T – Make 1 Twist - An increase by making a twisted loop over the right needle

P – Purl

Purl-wise – when picking up a stitch to the right needle enter it as if purling.

Pocket Style – Removing stitches from knitting needles to reveal a pocket.

PSSR – Pass stitch on right over left and off needle.

S – Slip Stitch – Enter loop on left needle purl wise and pass it to the right needle.

Single Row – Knitting individual rows rather than rounds

Single thread – Thread needle with one thread

sts – Stitches

Tail – The starting thread which remains when casting on stitches.

Tube Knit – After completing a row, do not turn work over. Slide work to right end of needle and carry feed thread along back side to begin a new row.

YO – Yarn over

Suppliers

To purchase supplies and knitted items from the author:

www.etsy.com/shop/miniaturesbyjoan

Threads

Danish Flower Thread

www.Scandinavianstitches.com
www.Hedgehoghandworks.com

DMC Embroidery Thread

Available at A.C. Moore, Michaels
or other craft needlework suppliers

Needles

0.70mm Knitting Needles
0.50mm Crochet Hook

www.hiyahiyanorthamerica.com

Printed in Great Britain
by Amazon